# FIRST BOOK

*of*

# PRACTICAL STUDIES

*for*

# TUBA

## FOREWORD

This FIRST BOOK OF PRACTICAL STUDIES is designed to develop chord consciousness and to provide additional experience in the fundamental rhythms, key signatures and articulations and to improve ACCURACY IN READING through the use of interesting and melodic studies. It may be used either to supplement or to follow any beginning method book.

When double notes occur in the studies, the E♭ Tuba will play the upper notes and the BB♭ Tuba will play the lower notes. Studies 1 through 16 may also be used to develop facility in reading and playing in "alla breve" tempo.

The following rhythms are introduced and developed in the First Book:

Scale studies, based on the keys introduced in this book, will be found on the following pages:

# FIRST BOOK OF
# PRACTICAL STUDIES FOR TUBA

## 1

## 2

E. L. 774

# 3

# 4

## 5

## 6

## 7

$1(\frac{1}{2})$

# 8

$0(\frac{1}{3})$

# 9

6

## 10

## 11

## 12

## 13

## 14

## 15

## 16

# 17

# 18

## 19

## 20

## 21

## 22

## 23

## 24

## 25

## 26

## 27

## 28

## 29

## 30

## 31

## 35

## 36

## 37

## 38

## 39

E.L. 774

## 40

## 41

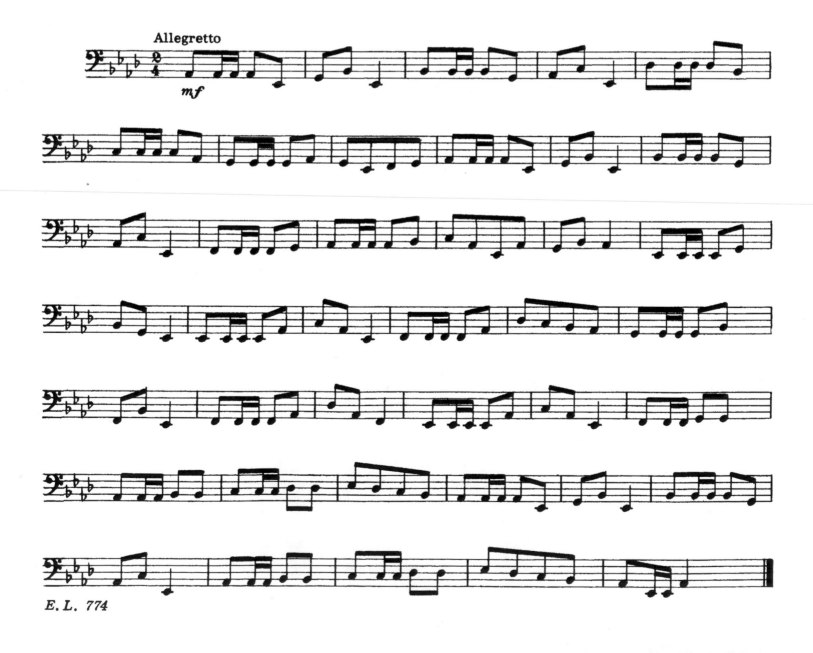

## 42

## 43

## 44

## 45

# 46

# 47

E.L. 774

## 48

## 49

## 50

## 51

Scherzando

## 52

## 53

## 54

## 55

## 56

## 57

## 58

## 59

## 60

# TECHNICAL EXERCISES

## ON THE MAJOR SCALES

E. L. 774

# CHROMATIC EXERCISES

# MAJOR SCALES
## DIATONICALLY AND IN 3rds